unspeakable. Only mothers who have experienced such a loss can truly understand the depth of the pain of losing a child.

Many blessings to Sandra Wilkerson who shared with the readers her bittersweet story of losing her precious child. Her story has brought comfort and peace to many who have suffered the agony of losing a child. In addition, Sandra Wilkerson has shared with the reader her unrelenting faith and belief in God during the most painful crisis of her life.

Mrs. Wilkerson has undeniably triumphed over the tragedy that changed her life and overwhelmed her in the wake of the death of her youngest daughter, Dee Dee."

—Jean Traylor Henson
Author

Thank you for your support.
Sandra K. Wilkerson

Memoirs of a Teenage Angel

Comfort After the Storm of Losing My Dee Dee

SANDRA K. WILKERSON

Belleville, Ontario, Canada

Memoirs of a Teenage Angel

First printing: February 2009
Second printing: August 2009
Third printing: April 2010

ISBN: 978-1-55452-357-3

For more information or to order additional copies, please contact:

Sandra K. Wilkerson
135 Boulder Creek
Desoto, TX 75115
sandrakwilkerson@yahoo.com

Guardian Books is an imprint of *Essence Publishing,* a Christian Book Publisher dedicated to furthering the work of Christ through the written word. For more information, contact:

20 Hanna Court, Belleville, Ontario, Canada K8P 5J2
Phone: 1-800-238-6376 • Fax: (613) 962-3055
E-mail: info@essence-publishing.com
Web site: www.essence-publishing.com

Dedication

I dedicate this book to God, Who is the head of my life. I never could have made it without You and all Your favor. I've been through the valley. I've been up and so very low. You took me through the heartaches, the pain and the storms when I could see no way through. You let me know that You were there for me. You had more faith in me than I had in myself. I'm stronger now. You've given me freedom from the bondage of sorrow of not having my Dee Dee here with me. You have given me a new vision of recovery, a new beginning, and it's all because of You letting me experience the unexpected. You promised me in Your holy Word that if my ways please You, You will not hold any good thing from me.

I thank You for allowing my family and me to be a part of the world's utmost ministry—

Full Gospel Holy Temple—under the leadership of the honorable Dr. Apostle Lobias Murray and his lovely wife, Dr. Shirley Murray. I count it an honor and a privilege to be under this ministry. It's my heartfelt prayer that You will richly bless them for the work that they have invested in our lives. We love and appreciate them more than they might ever know.

To my beloved husband, Joe B. Wilkerson Sr., whom I love dearly: Your love has given me strength through what we shared together. Because of our love, I know that we can conquer anything together. I love you so much.

Thanks to my lovely daughter, Nicole, for your precious time that you spent with me in helping me collect my thoughts while editing my book. Thank you for your patience and your love. I love you, and I'll always be there for you.

Thanks to my five wonderful sons: Joe B. Wilkerson Jr., Solon Duane, Cedric Charles, Dion Olaf and Kenan Drion, for the love and support that you have given me through the years. Your love for me keeps a smile on my face.

We are especially proud of our grandchildren and grateful for the pure pleasure of having them in our lives. We love you so much.

To Mr. Sherwood Blount and Mrs. Phyllis Marvill, we want to express our appreciation for your love and support and the generosity that you showed to our family during our time of sorrow in the loss of our daughter Dee Dee. We will always hold your friendship in our hearts. Your kindness shall always be remembered. May God bless you.

A special thanks to Clifford Ann, my sister and dear friend. You have always been there for me and my family. I love you.

A special thanks to my dear friend Linda Jackson for your love, your prayers and your assistance when I needed it most. You've been there for my family throughout our lives.

A special thanks to Mrs. Jeanette Williams, Mrs. Sharon Murray Smith, Mrs. Dorothy Farley and Mrs. Bobbie Brown for your support and for understanding what every tear was for.

Table of Contents

Preface

Dear Readers,

There's a story behind my praise. It tells how the Lord delivered me from my yesterday sorrow of losing our daughter and how I survived with help that only the Lord could give me. I hope that my book will become a lifeline for grieving parents. I pray that you can visualize the story and see the glory. It was difficult for me to believe that it would find its way to paper, because grief that besets a bereaved parent cannot adequately be put into words—but I'm so thankful that it did. It took a lot out of me and stirred up every emotion possible. Oftentimes, I had to stop because I couldn't bear the pain anymore. I would cry from all the memories brought forward.

I'm sharing some of the encounters that happened to me personally in my relationship with God. He has taught me how to trust Him with my whole heart, leaning not to my own understanding (Proverbs 3:5-6). When you are at the point of "what should I do?" and when all words have been spoken, the Lord will be your resting place. If you look to Him from which cometh your help (Psalm 121:1-2). You can have peace in the midst of your storm.

Sometimes the storms in your life can be so very discouraging, and it seems like you can't survive or make it through; nevertheless, I want to encourage you and let you know in order to have peace you must learn to trust in God. He can turn your tears of despair into a heart of peace and comfort when you look to Him as the Author and Finisher of your faith (Hebrews 12:2). Regardless of how dark it is, the sun is going to shine again, and everything is going to be all right after a while. You too can experience an added measure of strength and peace, and time will take you to a brighter day.

Psalm 34:4 tell us, "*I sought the LORD, and he heard me, and delivered me from all my fears.*" Mark 9:23 says, "*If thou canst believe, all things are possible to him that believeth.*" Oftentimes frustration can make you act before it's time. Be encouraged; don't give up; the storm will pass over after a while.

Only God knows what He has in store for you, and you must remember there's somebody who needs you to survive. I could see no ending to my broken heart. The Lord came in and quieted my spirit, teaching me how to trust and believe in Him to bring me out of what I thought was my impossible situation. I believe that you will understand my praise after you've read what the Lord has brought me through.

Trusting in God and drawing near to Him can turn a devastating situation into a life of purpose with joy, peace and happiness that surpasses all understanding (Philippians 4:7). God already knows our circumstances.

His concern is how we respond to those circumstances, and all He wants is for us to put our faith and trust in Him. We know that in our darkest hour, God's presence was there for comfort and strength. God is omnipotent.

We have our beloved daughter's lovely memories as solace for our grief; we pull together in Christ. No one knows how painful an experience the loss of a child is unless you have been there. When I look back over the years, so many memories fill the mind: the hope, joys, tears, sorrow, laughter and love we have all shared. Good things happen as a result of the Lord's tender mercies. I won't let a day go by without praising the Lord, and I give Him all the glory and honor that He so richly deserves.

I pray that each of your prayers will be answered according to your expectation. There's healing for your body and your mind and all of your brokenness. I know that prayer and praises will shake the foundation of your problem, and I believe that God has miracles to meet your needs.

I will rejoice and praise God with my voice for the mighty works that I have seen as Jesus keeps me near the cross, for that's where I want to be. I ask for grace to serve Him for the rest of my life as I continue to expect greater things from Him. I hope that my experiences will be as much a blessing to you as they were to me. I feel that this is a wonderful work from my heart. It's my prayer that our memories of my Dee Dee will direct people not to me, but to the one I serve—Jesus Christ, my Lord and Savior, and the Son of the True and Living God.

The Beginning of the End

It was a very special day for Dee Dee and her classmates. There was a special evening program scheduled at her school, Lobias Murray Christian Academy. She had informed us of her involvement throughout the program, how she had acting parts in the play and that she would be singing with the school choir as well as with a group of her peers. She loved to sing and spoke often of singing with the heavenly choir when she got to heaven. After returning home from work we were all rushing, preparing to return to her school for the program. She was so excited, and she didn't want to be one minute late. They had practiced long and hard for this occasion, and now they were ready to give it their best.

After arriving at the school, we found excitement was everywhere. The program was starting and all was going well. The first part was coming to an end. Dee Dee and some of her classmates rushed out the side exit door of the auditorium in order to return to the dressing room to change for their next performance. In their haste, Dee Dee slipped and fell from the sidewalk into some hedges. Unfortunately, the fall kept her from participating in the rest of the program. At the time, we thought she was more hurt mentally than physically.

After all the activities were over and we had returned home, she was very disappointed but seemed to be all right; but as I observed her closely through the night, I could see a change taking place that concerned me. She wasn't resting well and it seemed that she wasn't feeling well, but she never complained about anything. I decided to take her to the hospital emergency room to see exactly what was wrong. I told her my plans.

I left her older sister, Nikki, with her as I hurried to my bedroom to prepare for the trip. Suddenly, I heard Dee Dee call for me as if she was in excruciating pain. I rushed back to her room to see about her. To my surprise she was very calm. When she saw me, she began to pat the bed with her hand while saying to me, "Mama, sit down; sit down, Mama." Her soft voice was just above a whisper. I knew I needed to get her to the hospital, but I sat down anyway. She began to pull herself into my lap. I assisted her in doing so while explaining what I needed to do. She began to rock herself back and forth. I realized she was very weak, so I began to rock with her to make it easier. She seemed so calm. It was hard to believe that she was screaming for me a minute ago. I gently laid her back on her pillow. I knew that something was wrong, and I wanted to find out what it was.

I rushed back to my room to finish preparing myself. Again I heard her scream out for me. As I hurried back, I met her sister. I could see tears in Nikki's eyes as she was telling me to hurry and get Dee Dee to the hospital because her little sister looked as though she was dying. With resentment, I told Nikki that Dee Dee was not dying and that she would be okay—I just needed to get her to the hospital.

I was upset with Nikki for saying that. Dee Dee's dying had never crossed my mind. I didn't know at the time that they had talked and she had said her good-byes to Nikki and had told her that she loved her very much and that she knew that she wasn't going to make it to the hospital.

Again, I was standing by Dee Dee's bedside. Again, she was very calm. She began to pat the bed as she had done before. With her voice just above a whisper she said, "Sit down, Mama; Mama, sit down." I sat down. It was as if I couldn't refuse her. Again, she tried to pull herself into my lap. She wasn't strong enough, so I reached out and pulled her to me; with my help she began to rock herself back and forth as if she was a baby and didn't have a care in the world. All she wanted was her mother's love. I gently laid her head back on the pillow, praying all the while. I called out to her older brother to assist me in getting her to the hospital emergency.

I was partly holding Dee Dee as we traveled so that I could monitor her pulse. By then I knew that something was seriously wrong with my daughter. Upon arriving at the hospital, I could see people standing outside in the emergency area, and they could tell that something was wrong by the way we entered. Some of them began to open our car doors, trying to help while asking us what was wrong…what had happened…when…where? Some got in the car to check her vital signs while others hurried away to get a gurney. Soon they were taking her away as I began to explain to the doctors about her accident at school.

Afterward, I went to the hospital chapel to pray for a miracle. Sadly, it was not to be. After doing all they could do to save Dee Dee's life, they returned with the sad news that our daughter had died. As I listened, my heart felt like it was going to explode with pain. We were devastated and could not believe what we were hearing.

They led us to the room where Dee Dee was lying on the hospital bed looking as if she was only asleep. We were allowed to spend some private time with her. I will never forget that hour. I stood there with such disbelief, weeping and staring down at my child, observing the imprinted marks of life-saving attempts that covered her upper body. I began to pat them, as if to ease whatever pain that might have been caused from the pressure of it all, while saying, "No! No! No!" over and over again. I began placing kisses of love all over her face, trying to bear the unthinkable, trying to control the unbearable pain that had taken a powerful grip on my heart. If only I could bring back yesterday and make this awful moment disappear. To refer to my child as being dead was so difficult and unbearable. With all hope gone, I knew that it was true. I had to accept the fact that my Dee Dee was no longer with us.

A few hours ago she was so happy and excited; we all were. Now I'm trying to hold on to the broken pieces of my heart, asking myself repeatedly, "What could have possibly happened? How can this be?" It all happened so suddenly. So much was rushing through my mind. I asked the Lord, "How could You trust us with such a test of our faith? She was with us today, and today she is with You in heaven."

In my mind, He clearly spoke to me, "Yes, and she is a teenager also." As if to say "Remember?"

Immediately, I remembered. Everything came rushing back to me. As I reminisced over Dee Dee's last days, I realized it was the beginning of the end of our lives with her. I began to understand everything more clearly. In the midst of my misery and all the pain, I began to remember our Saturday morning talks concerning her petition that she had before God. Many of these conversations took place while we prepared the family breakfast. She had decided that she wanted to be a young person in heaven and to be a teenager throughout eternity.

At this time, she was already a teenager. She was thirteen years old. As I listened to her, I realized that she was very serious, and my heart became troubled. Oftentimes I tried to change the subject, but it would always come back to her petition. At first I didn't have very much to say, so I listened. The more she talked about it, the more disturbed I became. I was in disbelief. There were times when I was completely speechless. I really didn't know what to say, and even then it was hard to hold back the tears.

She continued with how she had prayed and asked God to come for her at a time that was most convenient. She was leaving it up to Him. She explained that she had prepared herself according to the Word of God. She knew that she was a Christian, saved and filled with the Holy Ghost. She was a believer of His holy Word, and she was going to keep herself ready by the grace of God and the power of the Holy Ghost. She had been taught how to live holy and how to live right before God in this present world. She was ready, and she knew that it could happen at any time because she was already a teenager.

I could no longer hold back the tears. I was asking God why my daughter was talking to me on this order. She had her whole life ahead of her. I just did not understand.

She went on to say that she knew that God hears and answers prayer and the Bible teaches that we must be born again and live a Christian life, pleasing unto God. If you have faith in Him you can believe Him for whatsoever you have need of, and He will give you your heart's desire. She knew that she had the faith. She had been taught faith through the Word of God by our leaders Apostle Lobias and Evangelist Shirley Murray, whom she loved dearly. She believed that she had all the faith that she needed, and she also believed that God was not going to disappoint her.

I could feel the pain growing inside of me. I was experiencing a new kind of hurt. It was as if I could feel the death of my child in my heart while she was alive and standing before me. I tried to control myself, but I couldn't. Her sincerity was so strong.

With tears streaming down my face, I tried to reason with her by bringing to her attention the many things she would miss if she left us so soon, being so young. Things like her high school and college graduations, getting married and having her own family, events that would take place in her sister's and brothers' lives that she would be happy about and want to be a part of. Her answer to me was, "But Mom, there's nothing that can compare to being in heaven with Jesus and singing in His heavenly choir; that's what I'm looking forward to."

The last Saturday morning that we spent together was the most painful of all. I knew that Dee Dee wanted to talk again. I didn't want to discuss it any more. My heart had suffered enough. I was tired of being stressed from it all. It had gotten to be too unbearable for me. And for what? She was still here with us. I thought with time this too would pass. But of course, she picked up our conversation where we had left off before. This time she was more intense with what she was saying. It was as if she was in complete control of the situation. She had checked and double-checked herself. She was ready for takeoff. Now all she had to do was wait on God.

Once more, my tears begin to flow. My heart was breaking into pieces. I could hear the conviction in her voice and see it in her expressions. It was as if she knew exactly what she was talking about and had no doubt that it was coming to pass. She knew that her time with us wasn't going to be long, and it was important to her that I understood things from her point of view. But I did not understand and I did not want to think of losing her under any circumstances. I could not imagine my life without her, and I didn't want to entertain the thought of her dying. As she continued on, it was not like having a conversation with my thirteen-year-old daughter any more. It was as if an angel was speaking to me through her.

As I cried the more, it was as if Dee Dee had noticed for the first time that I was crying and she came over to comfort me, giving me hugs and gentle pats on the back. She told me that she loved me and was not trying to hurt me and that everything was going to be all right. It was like her interest had turned to me and my personal feelings and how it was affecting me. She began to tell me that she knew that we were going to miss her and that it wasn't going to be easy for me. She knew that we were going to be terribly hurt. She wanted me to always remember that God would be there for me and He would be with us at all times. She asked me to trust in Him, because He was going to help me through it all and He would make everything all right, and it was important for me to remember that.

She was speaking to me as if she knew that I was going to need extra-special attention. She went on to explain that she was telling me before time because she wanted to prepare me for her home-going to be with God. She asked me to be happy for her, because this was going to be the happiest day of her life, and she wanted to have shared it all with her mom and how it all came about. It was important to her that I keep her memories fresh in the minds of her family and for them to remember that soon we will all be together again, because she believed that Jesus was soon to come for us all. All the while, I was asking God to help me bear all these sayings as I pondered them in my heart.

Three days later, the accident occurred at her school, and she did not survive her injuries. The doctors informed us that she had suffered a ruptured spleen from her fall, and a ruptured spleen could not be repaired. The Lord had granted her her petition. He carried her home to be with Him.

Now I'm feeling the reality of my pain and suffering. I know what it is to be paralyzed with sorrow and stricken with grief. This pain is like no other pain. She didn't go alone; a part of me went with her. It's so hard to let her go. Our private bonding times will always be very special to me now, and I will always remember all that she said. I admire Dee Dee for her bravery, her courageous stand of faith in God and for the love that she had for Him above all others. I feel proud for her to have such a petition before God and to have the faith to see it through to the end. There are times when I don't know what to do with myself, the pain is so great.

I thank God for blessing me to feel His holy presence and for being there to see us through these most difficult times ahead. There is no greater love than the love of God and to know that you are His child. Hebrews 13:5-6 tells us that He will never leave us or forsake us and He is our helper. I am so thankful to God for honoring Dee Dee's faith. I can almost hear Him say, "Welcome home, My good and faithful servant." She is now living in heaven with Jesus as a teenager, and it's for eternity. We, her family, are looking forward to that great day when we can all be together again; and what a day of rejoicing that will be!

No Tears Today

I was going about my day the best that I could, praying for relief as usual from what had me so burdened within. I was missing Dee Dee so terribly much. Just thinking about her began to cause a burning, stinging sensation in my face. I had never experienced anything like it before. Where was all this pain coming from and why was it affecting me in so many different ways? I began to rub and pat my face to help ease the pain away.

I thought, "Another misery added to all the other pain that I was already struggling with." I kept asking myself, "How can I get past not having my child in my life?" Oh how I wanted to hold her close and tell her how much I loved her as I had done so many times when she was here with me! Now I had to respect and accept her greatest and her last request to God that she would ever make—to live with Him in heaven as a teenager.

Now that He has honored her request, I'm trying so hard to understand it all. I know that God will not leave me in this state of being. God had more for me than merely existing, not only from day to day, but also from hour to hour. He has to come to my rescue. I don't know when and I don't know how, but I know that I am too desperate to be denied. Dee Dee assured me that He would be there for me and be my source of strength and my help in these trying times. I can't think of a time in my life when I have ever needed the Lord like I do now.

I could feel my face swelling from the hot tears that were filling my eyes, getting ready to flood my face again. Then suddenly, I felt the presence of God. It was like a cool chill that came over me, and in my way of thinking He spoke softly to me as if He was feeling my pain, telling me, "You will not cry today."

Immediately the tears were gone, so much so that not one tear fell from my eyes. I didn't feel the need to cry.

I knew that the Lord had visited me. He replaced my crying with praises and my heart was filled with Thanksgiving. I went about my day praising God for helping me to rise from my loneliness and despair. My burden seemed impossible for me, but I already knew that God is the Master of every situation and all He wants me to do is put my faith in Him and trust Him to be there for me. I knew He wasn't going to disappoint me. Dee Dee had assured me when she was preparing me for her home-going to heaven that He would take care of me. I'm seeing things more clearly now and from her point of view. I'm so grateful for this day, because God is letting me feel His great source of strength and His holy presence in my hour of pain and weakness. With all my heart I believe that He has just begun to prove Himself to my family and me.

Immediately After Dee Dee's Death

I was having a very difficult time coping with Dee Dee's death. Just the thought of getting over losing her frightened me, and it seemed impossible. I couldn't see an end to all this suffering; could all this grief ever go away? I besought the Lord for His mercy and His grace. I prayed that God would lead me to someone who I could relate to, who knew from experience what I was going through. I've been crushed with horror and stricken with grief and unbearable pain. If I could talk to a mother who had suffered the loss of a child, then perhaps she could give me some input on how the Lord healed her broken heart and how I could, too, endure such pain. There are times when only a mother's love can understand our disappointments. I needed peace of mind and my broken heart put back together again.

I searched but I could find no one. I needed a supernatural deliverance in my life. I needed to know how to stand my test of time. I desperately wanted to take my heart and place it in a safe place for a while so that I might get some relief from all the hurt that was inside. I believe that God is the Master of all impossibilities and prayer means talking to God and God talking back to you. The Word of God teaches us that we should always pray and not faint (Luke 18:1).

I would try to pray, but to concentrate on anything other than the pain of losing our child was almost impossible. Prayer will always be a very important part of my life because I know that prayer and having faith in God changes things. So many times I'd whisper a prayer to God to keep my composure when people were around or approaching us to show their love and give their condolences for our loss, but it was impossible. I would lose my self-control because the pain was so unbearable. Sometimes I would observe the people around me who seemed so happy. I would ask myself, "How can this be? How can they be so happy when I'm hurting so bad?"

I was indeed very pitiful and low in spirit. No matter who I talked to or counseled with, my heavy burden would always remain with me. It was like a dark shadow that refused to go away. The reality of losing Dee Dee was more than I could bear alone. I needed help, help that only God could give me, but I had to trust Him. I needed His grace and mercy; I needed it now. I needed Him in an extra-special way. There has to be a place in God where I could find peace and rest for my burdened soul. I needed to know how to survive my test of strength.

I began to ask Him for guidance to lead me there. I prayed that my faith would not fail me. I realized that nobody could restore me but God. He already knew all about my situation and what every tear was for. He had to have an emergency exit just for me.

When I made up my mind that I was going to let Him be my source of strength and my help, when I surrendered my all to the Lord, miraculous things began to happen. He began to prove that He was indeed my very present help in my time of trouble (Psalm 46:1). I found Him to be my great deliverer. He was there waiting on me all the time. As I sat in my bedroom chair, oftentimes pouring my heart out to God, trying to think things through, I would ask myself, "How long can my heart bear all this pain? When will I be able to smile and laugh again, and will it be the way that I really feel in my heart?"

It seemed so far from me if it could happen at all. How do you get over the death of your child? Dee Dee had been a part of my life for thirteen years. Carefully I would fold my arms, and in my way of thinking I would place myself in the arms of Jesus. I would rock myself as if He was rocking me so as to comfort His hurting child. As the tears flooded my face, I would tell Him again and again how much I loved Him; that I loved

Him more today than I did yesterday; that I wasn't angry with Him for carrying Dee Dee home to be with Him. He knew how much I loved her; I also knew that He loved her first. I wanted Him to know that everything was well with my soul.

Jesus would comfort me by bringing songs to my mind that I loved. I knew that He was speaking directly to me. Songs like "Stop by here, Lord, somebody needs you." I would answer, "It's me, O Lord, standing in the need of prayer." Another song was "I must tell Jesus—I cannot bear the burden alone." It was as if He was speaking life into my soul. I knew that He was with me. I could feel His presence all around me. I know that Jesus will talk to you if you have the time to listen, even at this time in my life, when it seemed as if my world had turned upside down. By His grace and mercy and by the help of the Holy Ghost, I knew that He had an emergency exit just for me.

Losing a child has to be the most devastating trial that any parent can possibly experience, and that kind of death has to be your worst enemy. Letting go of Dee Dee and moving on with our lives wasn't easy to do. I did things that may seem foolish to some. There were times when I would go to her closet and remove one of her garments and hold it close to me just so I could smell her scent. Somehow it made me feel as if I still had a part of her with me. I was desperately trying to hold on to her in whatever way I could.

I wanted so badly to be stronger for our other children. I didn't want them to see me like this, sad and crying all the time. But to be in their presence reminded me that Dee Dee wasn't here with us. Sometimes we would try to reminisce about her life, maybe something she said or something that she had done. It would always end up with us crying and consoling each other. She left us beautiful memories, but also sorrow too great to be told. We were all suffering the same kind of pain.

Once while observing the children, a quick thought went through my head. It was as if I was directing a question to myself. "We only had two daughters, but we have five sons; why not one of our sons?"

The Lord spoke two words to me; He asked, "Which one?" I immediately came back to reality with a sorrowful heart for even thinking such a thought. For a moment I had lost my focus, and it frightened me. I love all of our children and would not have wanted to part with any of them. I'm so thankful that it was God's decision. He already knew that she was ready and waiting on Him to come for her. We are thankful for the thirteen years that we were blessed to have her as a part of our big, happy family.

Growing up in a Christian household environment made a huge impact on how we all got along and the love that we had for one another. It's so hard to say good-bye to yesterday. God knows that I will always praise Him through the good times and the bad. I will always praise Him in all that I go through. It's not "if" I'm coming out; it's "when" I'm coming out.

March 28, 1985—Thursday Night Preparing for Church Service for the First Time

Preparing for church service for the first time since the death and burial of our beloved daughter Dee Dee was indeed a severe test of our strength. The pain was always present, like a thick cloud all around. There was no way to escape it. Being strong for my family was a challenge for me and did not come easily. I could barely hold my head up sometimes because the burden was so heavy on me. Our other children were concerned about their father and me. They watched us closely and often asked if there was anything that they could do for us. Knowing that they were feeling the same hurt that we were feeling was another concern of mine; of course, they knew that their sister had died and was no longer with us, but some of them were quite young and did not fully understand what we were going through. This was truly a very difficult time in our lives; however, it was now time for us to return to our regular church services.

I was trying my best to get myself together mentally as well as physically. This burden was like no other burden. It was impossible for me to bear it alone. All the while I was praying that the Lord would help me through this period of time in my life. Somehow I knew that He would. I knew that He would not leave me now. Returning to church and being among all the people was going to be another challenge for me. Sometimes being around other people can make you feel better, but at this time it was hard for me to talk to anybody without letting my true feelings come through. I tried so hard to control my emotions, but grief would always get the best of me. There were too many reminders that Dee Dee was no longer with us.

As I continued to prepare for church, I paused to look at her picture that I had placed on my dresser. In my mind I began to tell her how awful life was without her and that I had not experienced such hurt and pain before in my life. If only she knew how much I wanted her safely home. "If only you knew."

To my surprise, her picture had a special glow about it. Her soft voice entered my mind; she began to speak to me, saying, "Mama, I'm not coming back. I'm happy in heaven with Jesus, and I'm not coming back," as if she knew that I was struggling with the reality of not having her with me and accepting that she's never coming home. She went on to say, "You had better get your act together, because I'm waiting on y'all.".

I knew in my spirit that the Lord had visited me, and I looked around to see if her dad had been observing me. I knew if he had, he would know that something out of the ordinary had taken place. He had been busy preparing himself for church, so I pondered in my heart to share with my family some other time, but within myself, I was praising God all the way to church.

I was already into my own praise service when we arrived. I was praising Him for letting His tender mercy and amazing grace be with me. As I amplified my praise, I was blinded by my tears and the Lord began to bless me the more. I realized the more I reached out to Him, the more He drew nearer to comfort me. He was letting me know that He loved me and that everything was going to be alright; that our days would not always be cloudy and full of sorrow. Dee Dee had already told me that I could not imagine all the blessings that He had in store for our family.

I was so grateful for His visitations, yet deep within I was hurting and heartbroken. This burden was so hard to bear. If only I could find a starting place to recovery. I wondered when I would overcome this pain. Was it even possible? I know that the Lord has His own way of comforting us. He has a way of making you feel like there's nobody in this world but Him and you. When I think of the goodness of God and all that He has done for me, it gives me comfort in knowing that He is there for me just as Dee Dee had said that He would be. I love Him with all my heart and above all others. I appreciate Him for leaving His high, mighty throne in glory to come into this world and pay the awful sin debt so that we could repent of our sins and be saved. I've asked myself, "Who wouldn't want to serve an awesome God like Him"? I know that falling in love with Jesus is the best thing I've ever done.

Friday, March 29, 1985— Unbearable Hurt Taken Away

Today my husband called to tell me that he had something to share with me when he arrived home from work. I was looking forward to talking with him because lately it seemed as if there wasn't much to talk about. Our home was unusually quiet, even though we still had six other children. Everybody shared the same hurt and sorrow of losing Dee Dee.

While sitting down to dinner that evening, he began to tell me all about his day at work, how that he had become overwhelmed by the grief of losing our daughter and he felt that it would help him to go to the men's room to have a good cry. Afterward, while washing his face and preparing to return to work, he looked in the mirror. Suddenly he could hear the voice of Dee Dee as she began to talk to him in his mind, saying to him exactly what she had said to me the night before while preparing for church service.

She told him that she was happy in heaven with Jesus and she wasn't coming back; that he had better get himself together because she was waiting on us. Immediately and out of the ordinary, he could feel the unbearable hurt and pain leave him. After giving praise to God, he returned to work, rejoicing within his heart because he knew that the Lord had visited him and had lifted the heavy burden of the unbearable heartache and pain that had weighed heavy upon him.

As he was sharing with me all that the Lord had done for him and the joy of it all, I could feel the presence of the Lord coming over me. Miraculously I felt a jolt in my body as a powerful force of strength took hold of my heart. I could feel the tightness of its grip as it was putting forth a great effort to dislodge something inside me. It began with many powerful pulls upward. The pulls were so forceful, I felt as if they were going to lift me from my seat at any time. As they continued, I could hear a loud flopping sound of something tearing loose from inside of me, and I could feel relief from its tight grip as it let go each time. I was fully aware of everything that was taking place, but I felt absolutely no pain or fear from what I was experiencing, just discomfort from all the pulling and tearing. There were four parts that pulled loose, and when the last of it let go, I could see a fine mist as it went upward toward the ceiling before vanishing before my very eyes. Without a doubt I knew that the Lord had visited me once again. I surely felt that He had performed a supernatural surgery on me. I could no longer feel the unbearable hurt, and all the pain that had taken control of my life had been torn out and lifted away into thin air, vanishing like a vapor.

Afterward, I understood what the pulling and tearing was about. The Lord had taken away the unbearable pain that kept me crying and praying to Him for help to get me from one hour to the next because the overbearing grief of losing our daughter was always present. Now He has given me my self-control back. As the Lord was giving me my deliverance, another miracle was taking place, because I was still aware of everything that my husband was sharing with me. I had not missed a word. He continued on to tell me how when Dee Dee had finished speaking to him, he knew that God had taken the unbearable pain and hurt away because the heavy burden of it was gone, just as He had done for me. We began to praise God together, giving Him all the glory for His goodness, His mercy and His amazing favor. Without those things, we know we could not have made it through the storm.

We are thankful and grateful for His miracle-working power and His great deliverance on our behalf. Some might say that God's miracle-working days are over. I beg to differ with you. You came too late to tell me that, because He has been working miracle after miracle for my family and me while helping us through the storm of losing our beloved daughter.

Now I could hardly wait to share with him all that the Lord was doing for me while I sat listening to how He had come to his rescue and delivered him. The Lord knew that we needed deliverance that only He could give. He knew that our hope was in Him.

He is our ever-present help in our time of need (Psalm 46:1). He's mended our broken hearts and put the pieces back together again. Our faith, our hope and our trust are in Him, and He has not disappointed us. The hurt of losing Dee Dee and knowing that she is no longer here with us is always present, but the Lord has taken the unbearable part of it away.

We know from experience that grief and sorrow from losing a loved one can paralyze you, and the heartache and pain can be unbearable. We also know that there is comfort in knowing that God is our deliverer. Let me encourage you to put your faith and trust in Him. Call upon Him, and oftentimes He will answer while you are yet calling. Out of all that we have been through, we still have the joy of the Lord deep within our hearts. He keeps proving Himself over and over again. We are so thankful for everything that He has done for us, and I believe that He is not finished blessing us yet. If it's early in the morning or late at night, whenever I call upon the Lord, He is always there. I agree with the songwriter who wrote, "The voices of a million angels cannot express my gratitude. All that I am and ever hope to be, I owe it all to Thee…Just let me live my life and let it be pleasing, Lord to thee, and should I gain any praise, let it go to Calvary."

DeeDee, age 3

DeeDee, age 5

DeeDee, age 9

DeeDee, age 10

DeeDee, age 12

DeeDee, age 13

DeeDee, age 13 and Nicole, age 16

First Dream/Trip to Heaven, July 10, 1985

March 19, 1985, was Dee Dee's home-going date that God had chosen for her. He granted her the petition that she had before Him. Now she is a teenager living in heaven, just as she had wanted to be, and life for me will never be the same. My life is so difficult without her. Knowing that she is never coming home again is so unbearable. I'm sure that she is very happy in her new home in heaven, and I believe that there is no place that can be compared to it. Now I'm trying to understand it all. Why did she want to leave us and her life here on earth so soon? If she only knew the pain and sleepless nights that her death has caused within my heart. I honestly believe that she knew exactly how it would be. This is why she went to great lengths to prepare me for this long journey ahead before she left us. She knew how much we loved her and that we would miss her.

It would give me great joy to hear her laughter, to see her smiling face and to hear her call me Momma again. I asked the Lord for wisdom, how to keep her near my heart and fresh in my memories. He is such an awesome God. He reminded me of how often that I dreamed. Some of them seem so real. Oftentimes when I dream, only the people that I am dreaming about are visible. Then there are dreams that are interactive in nature and we are laughing, talking and having fun. The more I thought about it, the more excited I became. To me, having a dream about Dee Dee would be like having a visit with her. I begin to pray about it. In the word of God (1 John 5:14-15), it tells me "*And this is the confidence that we have in him, that, if we ask anything according to his will, he heareth us: And if we know that he hear us, whatsoever we ask, we know that we have the petitions that we desired of him.*" Also, Mark 11:24 tells us, "*Therefore I say unto you, what things soever ye desire, when ye pray, believe that ye receive them, and ye shall have them.*"

The months of April, May and June came and went. I was still believing God for my dream. In no way had I become discouraged. I had made up my mind that I was going to wait on the Lord and continue to take a stand on His holy Word because I knew that the Word of God could not lie. He had already done so many miraculous things for me in the past, and I wasn't about to doubt Him now. I believed that I had faith to believe Him for whatever I had need of, and to me this was considered a desperate need. Tuesday, July 9th, the Lord proved Himself to me by letting me dream about my Dee Dee. It wasn't an ordinary dream.

In my dream, there was a part of me that was always awake and watched me as I dreamt. I saw everything as it took place, and I was praising God all the while because I knew that it was Him that was letting me dream. But I soon realized that it was not the dream that I had hoped for. I had a newspaper, and Dee Dee's picture covered one of the pages. As I looked at the picture, I began to feel hurt and disappointed, not that I wasn't thankful to God for my dream but because I wanted her to be as she was before she left us. I wanted to interact with her. I began to tell the Lord, "No, no, no! This is not the dream that I had hoped for." Immediately I awakened. I could feel the hurt and disappointment in my heart, yet I was excited because the Lord had given me a dream about my daughter.

I started my day by preparing for our regular Wednesday morning prayer service at our church. As I began to pray, I thanked the Lord for all that He had done for me and all that He was going to do. I also thanked Him for the faith to believe Him for the things that I desired of Him. I was being sure that I was making my request known. As time passed on and our prayer service was nearing the end, I began to thank God for my next dream.

The Spirit of the Lord came over me, and things began to happen. Suddenly, I was carried away in the spirit. My natural mind was no longer in the prayer service. It seemed as if I was in my body, but I must have been out of my body because I could see myself praising God in the prayer service. I was so amazed, but I never said a word. In my way of thinking, I asked myself what was the meaning of this. Within a blink of an eye, I was away and traveling among the clouds in the sky. What a beautiful sight to behold. Each of them had a silver lining that glowed. I could feel the softness of their gentle touch on my face as I passed through them. I didn't have any fear whatsoever as to what was taking place with me, because I knew that God was visiting me again. I knew I had to be somewhere in the heavens because of my surroundings. Everything was so peaceful, and I felt as though I didn't have a care in the world. I was so happy and excited. I was observing everything that I could see around me, and it was as if I could see miles and miles away.

As I continued to travel, I came upon the brightest light I had ever seen. It was in the form of a circle. It was extraordinarily large, and I couldn't see through it. It came across my mind, "Is this the throne of God?" It had to be, because I could feel and sense the presence of God all around me. I could see multitudes of people and they were all bowed as if they were praising God. They began to look like grains of sand because of the distance. I thought again, "Where am I?"

Coming from behind me, a male voice answered and said, "This is the throne of God." He already knew my thoughts. While I was observing this beautiful place and all the people around it, I was overwhelmed with admiration as I pondered it all in my heart. My being in the presence of God's throne was almost more than I could comprehend. Suddenly I thought, "If I'm in heaven, where is Dee Dee?" My heart was overflowing with joy and excitement. I knew that I was about to see my daughter.

With great anticipation, I began to look all around for her. She had to be there somewhere. Again, from behind me, I heard the same male voice call for her. "Dee Dee, Dee

Dee, show yourself, girl; your mother is looking for you."

At that very moment, I saw a beautiful white curtain as it was slowly being pulled back by Dee Dee. I watched as she stood there smiling, looking as excited to see me as I was to see her. I wish I could explain the feeling inside me as I saw my DeeDee. Being saturated with liquid joy is unexplainable. I noticed everything about her, including her facial features. Her complexion was as smooth as velvet. Her hair was beautiful, styled in her favorite hairstyle that she loved so much.

Again the male voice spoke from behind me, saying, "You know she has been changed." At this moment her attention left me. She began to look downward, and to my surprise, we could see all the way from heaven to earth. I could see she was observing me in our prayer service meeting. We could see everybody there. She never said a word, but I knew what she was thinking and it was as if I could hear her talking to herself. Her thoughts were "There's Momma in prayer service; yes, she'll be here soon." The expression on her face told me she was pleased because she could see I was making preparation to join her in heaven by living a life pleasing unto God. My thoughts came back to my request that I had before God. I began to praise Him for taking me on the most glorious, exciting trip of my life, a trip all the way to heaven for a personal visit with my daughter when I was only asking for a dream.

I immediately felt my spirit enter back into my body where I was standing in prayer service. It was like a powerful yet gentle jolt that took place. I was praising God in the spirit like I had never done before. I wish that I could express the magnificence of it all. It was a trip that seemed to have taken hours but it must have taken only a few seconds, because when I arrived back, they were still in the midst of dismissing prayer service. I can report to you of a truth that Dee Dee is in heaven with our Lord because He took me there to see her and to let me visit with her. She looked the same as she did when she left us to go home to be with Him.

Dee Dee's being a teenager in heaven has to be above and beyond her greatest expectations, and the joy in her expression explained to me just how happy she was to be there. The Lord had given me an understanding of everything that she was praying for and let me see her future with God as she desired it to be. I believe that she was very special and had high favor with God to ask such a petition and have the faith to see it through to the end. She is happy, and she will always be a teenager in heaven, and it's for eternity, just as she desired.

I consider myself blessed and highly favored of the Lord also because He accompanied me on my journey to heaven. I believe with all my heart that the male voice that spoke to me from time to time was that of Jesus. I could feel His compasion and love flowing to me each time He spoke to me. I believe it was the most amazing, powerful experience I have ever had. I'm so thankful and will forever be grateful for all His miracle-working power, for His unconditional love and for His tender mercy that He has shown to my family and me; however, the greatest miracle of all is when He saved me and filled me with His precious Holy Ghost. The Word of God tells us that our heavenly Father gives the Holy Ghost to them who ask for it. I asked, and He did not disappoint me. He made me a new creature in Christ Jesus. Second Corinthians 5:17 tells us that "*If any man be in Christ, he is a new creature: old things are passed away; behold, all things are become new.*" It is the Holy Ghost that enabled me to live a life that's pleasing unto God. I've learned not to lean to my own understanding but to His will as it is written in His holy Word.

The Lord will be to you whatsoever you need Him to be. Mark 9:23 tells me, "*If thou canst believe, all things are possible to him that believeth.*" He will withhold no good thing from you. Remember, Jesus loves you, and He doesn't want to see you in what seems like an impossible situation. He alone has power over every situation.

Believe what the Word of God says. As I

stated before, Mark 11:24 tell us, "*What things soever ye desire, when ye pray, believe that ye receive them, and ye shall have them.*" Prayer changes things, and oftentimes He'll answer you while you are yet calling. I waited patiently on the Lord. He has made known to me the ways of life, and every day is not going to be filled with sunshine. A little rain must fall sometime, but regardless of how dark it gets, the sun is going to shine again.

The Lord has given us our very own prayer line straight to Him, and it's never busy. I will continue to wait patiently on the Lord. He is proving to be the sweetest counselor, my resting place and my great deliverer. He has given me peace in the midst of my storm. My eyes have seen His mighty works and experienced His miracle-working power. Dee Dee said that He would be with me in the beginning even as He is with me now. He is no respecter of persons (Acts 10:34). It all happened to me after prayer.

The song "Willing" by Nancy Grandquist

perfectly portrays the way I feel in my heart and my relationship with God. It says:

My heart is listening for you, Lord.
Say the words and tell my what to do
So help me, Lord, I want to serve you
I hope you find something in me that you can use.
I'm willing to do everything I can
Willing to say yes when I don't understand
Willing when there is a price that must be paid
I'm willing to do anything that you say
Willing for the pain and loneliness I must bear
Willing to give you myself any place and anywhere
You see, Lord, today your child is willing
I already know that it won't be easy
And sometimes the road is going to be rough
It's no sacrifice for you
I don't see where living for You would be enough

You see your child is willing, and my heart is listening.

Four Months Later—Convocation Revival (July 1985)

Preparing for our convocation revival was always exciting to me because of the wonderful time that we would have while attending the many different church services throughout the meeting. We looked forward to seeing many of our friends who came from far and near. The Lord truly blessed in every service.

It's an exciting time for the young people as well. They loved dressing up and being with their friends, and Dee Dee was no exception. She had lots of friends. At this time, I had not seen many of them since her death, and seeing them was going to remind me that she was not here. In the past, it was always a joy to see them all as they came to me asking for her. But this year, I knew that they would be coming to see how I was doing out of respect for me and their love for Dee Dee. They missed her also, yet they were going to be careful how they spoke of her—trying not to add to an already sad situation. I was sure they would be able to see it in my countenance and hear it in my conversation that I was still struggling with the loss of my daughter and their friend. To see them would bring back memories that would take me too far back into the past. This meeting was going to be different and difficult for me this time.

I've had so much on my mind since the Lord has carried Dee Dee home to be with Him. It has been about four months now, and it's still very fresh on my mind and in my heart. I will always be grateful to the Lord for removing the unbearable pain from me, but the hurt of knowing she's gone and never coming back again remains with me. I miss her so much. Usually, at the beginning of our church service I would tell the Lord,

"Anyway you bless me, I'll be satisfied," but tonight I needed an extra special blessing with my name on it.

After arriving at church, as we stood for the opening of the evening services, we were asked to greet the person next to us by telling them that it's good to see you here. As I was about to do so, immediately the Lord carried me away in the spirit to heaven, and I knew I was there to see my Dee Dee. She was running to greet me, and I could hear the excitement in her voice as she called out to me, "Mama, it's good to see you here," as if she had been with me in our church service and was greeting me accordingly. I was caught up in the moment, and all the while I knew that God was doing something miraculous for me. At this time, I was feeling no hurt, and the joy of being with my Dee Dee made me feel as though I didn't have a care in the world. If only I could express to you this feeling of joy that was bursting inside me. Then suddenly, I was back in the midst of the people in our church service where the Spirit of the Lord was very high among the people praising God. It took me a while to come back to reality because the experience was so overwhelming.

Surely the Lord had given me a blessing with my name on it! A blessing that only He could have given me, and I felt so honored. Again, He had taken me to heaven to visit my daughter. I'm so thankful for the words of encouragement that she said to me, "It's so good to see you here," because sometime soon, heaven is exactly where I'm going to be. I've asked myself, "Who am I that God is so mindful of me that He visits me and makes me a part of His miracle working power?" The Word of God tells me in Hebrews 13:8, "*Jesus Christ the same yesterday, and today, and for ever.*" I'm so glad that He included me in His miracles of today.

Dee Dee did her best to prepare me for life after her journey home. She assured me that the Lord was going to be with us and that He was going to do great things for us. I could not have imagined such great things that He had in store. God has assured me that Dee Dee will always be a part of our lives. I'm trusting and watching for Him to bring it to pass. I love the experiences that He has given me with my daughter from His point of view. I will always offer thanksgiving from my heart, and His praise will continually be in my mouth. I feel blessed to have my days of visitation from the Lord. I'm convinced that only He can do such great things for my family and me.

I know that prayer can change your situation if you believe in God's Word; no matter what you are going through, God can make the difference. All He wants in return is your love above all others and for you to serve Him with your whole heart. Truly He is the source of my strength. He is the strength of my life, and when I couldn't see my way, He showed me a better way.

There are times when I offer praise to God, giving Him honor and thanks for all His divine favor in our lives. Then there are those times when I think of the goodness of God and all that He has done for me, and it causes an uncontrollable praise to pour from my soul.

Second Dream: "Limousine"

Once again I was talking to God, telling Him how grateful I am for all that He has done for me and for His continuous blessings. He already knew that I had a desire to dream about Dee Dee again, because He knows everything. I missed her so much. To see her smiling face, to feel her near me, would give me great joy and peace of mind.

As I retired for the night, it happened as it did many times before. As I laid my head on the pillow, I could feel myself entering into my dream. I knew that the Lord had come to my rescue once again. As before, I could see myself as I dreamed and began praising God.

I was sweeping inside my house. As I looked out, I could see a long, shiny car pull up and stop. I hurried to the screen door to get a better view of who it was that was coming to visit me. I wasn't expecting anyone. As I looked out, I could see that it was a long black limousine. It was beautiful. As I was admiring the car, the front door opened and a male uniformed driver stepped out and proceeded to walk hurriedly around to the other side of the car and opened the back door. Of course, he had my full attention as he took a young lady's hand and helped her from the car. I'm yet wondering, "Who could this be?" I couldn't see her clearly, because the driver was blocking my view. I watched as he turned himself about to help her get from the car to the steps that led to my door. Now I could see that this young lady was my Dee Dee!

I began to rejoice. I couldn't keep my composure. I began calling her name as I ran out to meet her as she came up the steps. She had the biggest smile, and I could see that she was just as happy and excited as I was. We began to hug and kiss each other. She never said a word, but she was laughing and laughing as I picked her up and began to take her around and around in a circle out of excitement. As I was doing so, I noticed she had no weight about her. She was as light as a feather. It didn't concern me; it just puzzled me for a moment, but our joy and excitement quickly erased the thought from my mind. We were together again, and that was all that mattered. I knew that she was visiting me from heaven, and that made the visit even more special. As I was praising God for His glorious works and for another dream with my baby, He quickly let me know that He let her come in style, in the finest, in a limousine, which was so awesome to me. She was as beautiful as she ever was. Dee Dee was truly a blessed child. I consider myself a very blessed Mother.

I realize missing Dee Dee will be part of my everyday life now. I sometimes reminisce on the conversations we had a few months before the Lord carried her home, as she was trying to prepare me for the long journey that awaited me. It seemed as if I didn't comprehend anything that she was saying. I know that it was because I didn't want to. I wanted to think that it was a waste of time and this phase in her life would soon pass; but it didn't. She kept on and on. Sometimes she would stop and comfort me when I couldn't hold back the tears. Even then it seemed so real. Sometimes there were rebuking tones of voice that she would use as to say, "Hear me, Mama, please hear me. Don't make light of what I'm saying." Then she would remind me of the goodness of God and how that He would always be there for me and that He would never leave me alone. To my surprise she added, "Mama, you are going to be just fine."

She always spoke with such confidence. I can truly say all that was said has been done, and it happened just as she said it would. God has given me an understanding to everything that she was so passionately trying to explain and was trying to protect me from. Life is not always easy, but He did not say that it would be. With lots of prayer, my faith in God and my love for Him above all others, I can say with assurance that I'm going to be just fine. All the glory and honor goes to God, who is the head of my life.

Third Dream: Flower Garden

I know how blessed I am to have the Lord in control of my life. I know that if I ask for anything according to His will, He hears me, and I know that I have what I desire of Him. Again, my desire was to dream about my daughter. There are times more than others when I want to feel near her. The Lord granted me my request.

After retiring for the night, I could feel myself entering into my dream. In my dream I was drawn to the living room window. As I looked out, I could see my beautiful Dee Dee, watering a garden full of gorgeous flowers. I watched as she cared for each of them. Everything about her was beautiful and perfect. Her hair was neatly in place and her skin was smooth like velvet. I was taken aback as I could not decide what was more beautiful, her or the flower garden. I knew that this was a scene from heaven. The grass was so green and the flowers were so perfect. Praising God seemed to be a continual thing for me. I praised Him for His goodness.

I knew that this was something out of the ordinary, and every time He proves Himself to me, it's a glorious reminder of Dee Dee preparing me for this long journey ahead and how that she told me that the Lord was going to do great things for me and that every day wasn't going to be tears of sorrow. I know that being in heaven with Jesus is where she wanted to be as a teenager, to be a teenager throughout eternity. Deep within my heart, I have great joy for her, but there is also guilt, knowing that I want her here with me.

Fourth Dream

A normal day for me after returning home from work was to start working all over again, preparing dinner for the family and supervising the kids as they prepared for school the next day. By 10 p.m., I was usually overwhelmed with fatigue, rushing to get everything done so I could have some quiet time to gather my thoughts of Dee Dee without interruptions. I would actually reach out as if to pull her into my lap. In my thinking, I would talk to her, letting her know how much I loved her and how much I missed her and how hard it was to say goodbye to yesterday. This was another way of keeping her close to my heart.

The Lord is so merciful. He is giving me wisdom by letting me know how far to let my mind travel back into the past; that way I can control some of the hurt that remains with me. Although the Lord took the unbearable part of the pain away, the hurt of not having her with us remains with me. There is a tremendous difference. I know that I have a long way to go to recovery, but with the Lord's help, I'm getting my life back in perspective. I'm seeing a wonderful change come over me, a spirit of peace and quietness from all my grief. I'm happy for her because I know she is happy and safe in her new home in heaven. I will always remember what she told me: "There's no place to compare with heaven." I believe her and I'm making it my business, by the help of the Holy Ghost, to join her there by living a life pleasing unto God. I can hardly wait to be with her in our new heavenly home, where I believe that it will always be "howdy, howdy, and never any good-byes."

While praying before retiring for the night, I asked God to give me another dream so that I could visit with her again. As I laid my head on my pillow, I could feel myself entering into my dream, and as before, I knew that it wasn't an ordinary dream. It was as if He had come for me Himself. I felt so very special because I knew that God was answering me while I was yet calling on Him. I knew that I was dreaming and in my dream I was watching myself as I dreamed. This time I heard a knock on my bedroom door; carefully, as not to disturb anybody and before I could answer, Dee Dee began to talk to me. With concern in her voice she said, "Mama don't get up," as if she knew how tired I was. She went on to say, "I stopped in to say hello and to let you know that I'm doing just fine; I'll talk to you later, okay?" I answered, "Okay." As she was leaving, I knew that the Lord had allowed her to come from heaven to visit me. This time it was even more special because He had let her talk to me. As I awakened, I continued on with my praise, for the overwhelming joy that I was feeling and for granting me another visitation with my daughter.

Today, I am fully confident that prayer changes things. I believe that nobody can do these acts of God but God. I'm excited and fully persuaded that He will always be there for me. He will comfort, strengthen and bring me out with the victory just like Dee Dee said that He would. I know that it is not all about me; its about the will of God being done.

"*The LORD is my strength and my shield; my heart trusted in him, and I am helped: therefore my heart greatly rejoiceth; and with my song will I praise him*" (Psalm 28:7). Maybe you can't understand my praise because you don't know what I've been through. I go to God time after time for comfort and care; it's because I believe that He understands me so completely. His love has carried me further than I thought I could ever go. He has taken me places that I have never dreamed of, and my life will never be the same. I don't know when or how He's going to bless me. I do know how grateful I am every time He does. I could go on and on and on because gratefulness keeps flowing from my heart.

Words of Thanks

We are grateful to our family, our church family and our friends. Words do not adequately express our sincere appreciation for the support you have rendered during the home-going celebration of our beloved daughter, Dawna Denise Wilkerson (Dee Dee). Whether you gave cards, flowers, food, made a monetary contribution, gave hugs or said a prayer, we are very appreciative. For those who loved her and befriended her during her lifetime, we are very grateful. For those of you who have lifted us and our family in her home-going, we are very blessed. Again your kindness shall always be remembered.

To Apostle Lobias Murray and Evangelist Shirley Murray, our leaders in the gospel for over thirty-eight years, you are the best leaders that we have known, and we love you dearly. God has used you to help guide, encourage and motivate us through the years, and when we were experiencing our darkest hour in the loss of our beloved daughter Dee Dee, you were there for us. It is my heartfelt prayer that the Lord will richly bless you for the work that you have invested in our lives. We love and appreciate you more than you will ever know.

I would like to give a special thank you to Laurese Murphy for her tedious help in bringing this book to fruition. Please know that I sincerely appreciate your efforts and pray God's continuous blessings upon you.

All About Me and My Family

My name is Dawna. My family consists of five brothers and one sister. Their names are Cedric, Dion, Kenan, Joe, and Duane, and my sister's name is Nicole (but we call her Nikki). We live in a four bedroom, two bathroom brick house. We live in Dallas, Texas. My brother and my sister are over me in age. He's twenty-one, she's sixteen. I'm only thirteen.

Well I'm going to tell this story the best way I can and tell it, from as long as I can remember.

First of all I can remember when there was no one but me, my sister, and my brother. They used to always boss me around (and they still try to now). Well anyway, a few years or so after that, my mother was pregnant (she always tell us a few months after). So when she finally told us, I was so excited. I thought, now I will have some one to push around too. It seemed as if it took a long time for the baby to come. Everyone wanted it to be a boy. I went around telling everyone that I was going to have a baby brother. I was so excited. Every day I would wake up and ask my mother if the baby had arrived yet. So one day, my father took me, my sister, and my brother over to my grandmother's, who lives a good five minutes away from us. I asked him why he was taking us over there. (I always talked a lot.) But he never told us. So I thought the baby was over there. So I could hardly wait. But when I got over there, it wasn't. So we stayed over there for about two nights, and finally my father picked us up. When we got home my mother was there and so was my new brother. I jumped in her bed and woke him up. I was so glad. I even wanted to sleep with him, but she wouldn't let me. We had so much fun even though my mother stayed in bed all week. We had so much company. I begged my mother every day to let me hold him but she said I had to be older. I cried. That was a very exciting time and I will always remember it. Anyway my next brother came up but I wasn't excited as I was at first. But this one took even longer but I expected it. I went out of town to my other grandmother's and aunt's house. When I came home back I had another brother. This time my mother let me hold him. I told all my friends. But I wanted a sister, but a brother was just fine. Our family began to increase and I stopped getting all the attention, and I began to get mad.

My First Day at School

My first day at school was the worst. I attended William Brown Miller for four years. It was a nice school and nice people were there. My first real experiment was there. When I had my first boyfriend. He's in my reading class now. I was good and ready to come home from school.

In November, I was at school. My mother came and picked me up. She told me she had a surprise for me. So I couldn't wait. When we got halfway home she had us to put our hands over our eyes. When we took them down there was a new car. I was surprised. That was another big experience.

My Last Two Brothers

My mother began to ask us if we wanted another brother. I said no, I wanted a sister. My oldest brother said she must be pregnant. But I didn't say anything. When she finally told me that she was pregnant again, I said it have to be a girl. But it wasn't. I really enjoyed my last two brothers. They were so spoiled (and still are). We had so much fun.

Now that everyone is five or older, things have changed. I miss not having a baby in the house. I always tell my mother to have another baby and maybe it will be a girl. She tells me, she has had all the children that she's going to have. But I still tell her that.

Some people say with a large family you can't have much, but I am here to say otherwise. My father spoiled me to death. I have everything I want, so does my sister and brothers. I really like my mother and father and the family I'm into. I can sit down and tell my folks my problem and they always seem to know the solution.

Now I'm waiting to become eighteen. These are the things I want to do:

Have my own place.

Have my own car.

Have my own money

I think that those are some pretty good reasons. I often tell my mother that and she tells me I'll be the last one there. But I think different. I think it's time for my oldest brother to leave because he's twenty-one. He needs to go and start a family, but it's fine having him around (sometimes). My sister can be a pest at times. She always does things that she knows make me mad. Not too long ago we had a fistfight. It was fun but it was also hurting me. When my mother found out, she put both of us on punishment. But now we know better.

Last month I had a birthday. August 28. I turned thirteen. (I was so glad. It seems like it took a long time to become a teenager, but I'm finally one.)

Well, this is about as long as I can remember. And also as long as I've lived. So now I go to Oliver Wendell Holmes (which is boring). I also like my old school better and wish I could go back. Well that's it.

The End

Dawna Denise Wilkerson
(Dee Dee)

Special Thoughts

Upon reading *Memories of a Teenage Angel* so many memories flooded my mind. The passing of my sister was the most devastating thing that I have ever experienced. I picked up the book with a heavy heart and began to read the unfoldings of that dreadful day. Unbeknownst to me, this book was about to revitalize, encourage and strengthen me. As I turned page after page my sadness began to turn into joy. I was able to read about the pain her death caused my mom, but at the same time, I was able to read about the goodness of God and how He brought her out with the victory! I remember watching my mother on many occasions as she went about her daily routine. I saw her smiling at us, but her eyes had lost their sparkle. I remember wondering if my mother would ever truly be happy again and praying to God asking Him to please give her eyes back their glow. As time went on, I slowly began to see the handiwork of the Lord upon her. I knew He was doing for her what no one else could do. Even though it took some years, I saw that sparkle come back into her eyes. Oh what a happy day that was for me. My mother didn't have anyone else to turn to at that time who really understood what she was going through, but thank God; now many people can turn to her for encouraging words, for truly she understands. Little did she know in 1985, God was going to take her through and bring her out of a fiery trial so that many years later she could be a blessing to others.

I miss my sister dearly, more so now than ever. I often wonder what malls we would shop at, what restaurants we would frequent, and the secrets we would share. I know we would have visited each other often; her kids definitely would have loved their Aunt Nikki (smile) and I know my son would have loved her. I have told him so many things about his Aunt Dee Dee. I came to realize that God had a higher calling on my sister's life. I also came to thank God for honoring her request and letting her be a teenage angel. I know she watches over me, as I have felt her presence many times. I give God all the glory for blessing my family during our toughest time and for getting us to where we are now. We are a close-knit family and we stand together no matter what: to God be the glory.

Mom, I love you and look up to you. You are truly a woman of extraordinary strength. How God must have loved all of us to give us a mother like you.

Nicole Wilkerson-Willis

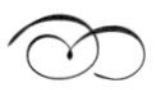

A Letter to My Best Friend

Hey Girl,

Whatcha doing, girl? Me, just sitting here thinking and remembering the good times we shared. Remember how we just couldn't wait for the convocation to begin. We would go to Bobby's T-shirt store and get our names put on our shirts, yours on mine and mine on yours. Of course we thought we were so cute with our T-shirts and blue-jean skirts on. Girl, we thought we were really doing it (smile). Nobody could tell us we weren't cute.

Dee Dee, on the more serious note, I miss you so much. Words cannot express the way I felt then and feel even now. I never question God's ways, but at first I just couldn't understand why you had to leave me. Of course I'm older now and I know why. I remember like it was yesterday when the Lord saved you that Sunday morning. You were so excited. After church you and I were standing at the street waiting for the traffic to pass so we could get across. You turned to me and said "Pooh, I

am ready to go to heaven now." I replied and said, "Girl, you are just excited, don't be talking like that. I know you want to go to heaven, but not now, and don't be talking to me like that." With your squeaky little voice you said, "Pooh, I am for real, I'm ready." Girl, not many days after our conversation at the church, the Lord took you home. It hurt so badly and all I could do at that time was cry. I cried many times at night because I missed the times you and I would talk, giggle and act silly on the phone. Even though my heart was so broken about you leaving me, I know God knew what He was doing and I respect God's decision. He knew you were ready to be with Him. Dee Dee, keep on looking down on me and my family and one day we will get to talk, giggle and play together again. Girl, I've gotta close now, because I'm teary-eyed trying to get through this letter to you. I miss you so much.
Love ya!

Your best friend,
Ingrid Brown (Pooh)

P.S. Dee Dee, I do get comfort when I see your niece Sydney. Guess what, girl, she looks just like you. I don't know if she has that squeaky little voice like yours. She probably thinks I'm crazy because when I see her, I just stare because she looks so much like you. I did hug her one day. I closed my eyes and my thoughts were of hugging you.

Dear Dee Dee,

It is not easy to lose someone who has been loved by so many. You were one of "us," being a student of the Lobias Murray Christian Academy (LMCA). We saw each other every day of the week because most of us attended the same church also. Saturday night and Sundays were part of our regular scheduled church services. I remember being one of many of your heartbroken and grieving friends sitting in the classroom where you once sat trying to understand everything concerning your accident that had taken you from us too soon. Reminiscing on the good times, we always come back to this sad moment, which is still so unbelievable. I miss you, Dee Dee. The sweet memories of us growing up together, attending school and church together will always be special to me and will live in my heart forever. You were a good friend, and I love you.

Tony Jackson
Former classmate

Some people come into our lives and quickly go…Some people stay for a while and leave their footprints on our hearts, and we are never ever the same. I remember Dee Dee with her infectious grin, bubbly personality and long thick ponytails. She was very intelligent and well-liked by all.

Nikki Jackson
Former classmate

As we progress in life, we come to understand that friendship is essential to the soul. On March 19, 1985, my soul was dealt a damaging blow when my friend, Dee Dee, died. For the past twenty-three years, I have thought of her quite often. I've thought about how we would talk on the phone while watching one of our favorite television shows, *Miami Vice.* I've thought about how we would laugh until our sides ached. I've thought about how she was very competitive and would recite the books of the Bible with lightning speed. Oh, who can forget her birthday, August 28th? So many memories come to mind, many of which involve Dee Dee, at some point, chewing her favorite chewing gum—Big Red. After she died, I found myself chewing Big Red gum when I would miss her (even though I didn't really like it!). But with the passing of time, I have come to smile when I think of her—no more Big Red and no more crocodile tears. Now I smile and thank God for gifting me with a friend that, after twenty-three years, is still so special that our friendship transcends time and mortality.

Tosha R. Sherman
LMCA Classmate

Dear Dee Dee,

Oh, how I miss you. I often think about you and the day that you left us. I think about how happy you must be in heaven right now and how I look forward to seeing you there one day. I am so grateful to God that He allowed our paths to cross, because you have impacted my life in such a positive way and left a lasting impression. I'll always love you, and I'll see you again one day.

Your friend and classmate
Marcia Francis Mallard

When I think of Dawna, I think about how she was such a caring child. How she would say things that made you feel good and made you feel good about yourself.

This is a book that you can read over and over again. You will cry, laugh and feel good inside. What a beautiful angel!

"Aunt" Linda Jackson
Full Gospel Holy Temple

Out of the twenty-nine years of my teaching career, there have been some students who stood out a little more than others. Dee Dee was one of those students.

Dee Dee made a lasting impression on me because before I even got a chance to teach her, she let me know how she felt about me and her coming to sixth grade.

To me Dee Dee was a student who I believe that all teachers would have loved to have in their class. I say this because she had a wonderful personality and a beautiful smile, she was very smart and loved school, she was a hard worker who loved to laugh. She also loved to write me letters. Dee Dee always had something to say to me.

During the time that I had her in my class, she became one of my top students and she was also a very good helper.

Dee Dee will always have a special place in my heart, and I am looking forward to seeing her smiling face once again in heaven.

Ms. Barbara Haggerty
Former Instructor, Lobias Murray Christian Academy

Dear Dee Dee.
Dawn Denise Wilkerson

Oftentimes I find myself thinking of you and wishing among wishes that you were still here. I know that in spirit you are; yet it's the beautiful smile and laughter of the physical self I deeply miss. I sometimes see a candle's flame and how it brightens up a room, and then I see you—how you brightened up my every day. Some called it a schoolyard crush but I call it a best friend-"girl"-family. I look at your mom as my second mom and Nicole as my sister and then I see you in their beautiful faces, smiles and laughter. But just like in school, you made it to the finish line before me; yet rest assured I'm coming to get heaven's trophy as well. One of these days we'll laugh, talk, sing and rejoice amongst the heavenly host. Thanks for watching over your friend and brother. I'll love you always as you rest in the bosom of Jesus.

Love your "Brother"
Rodney De' Shun Jackson Choice
P.S. My daughter is named after you, "Dawn" Denise—Zaquera "Dawn"

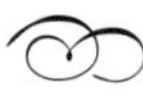

Dear Dawna,

I must say that I was in total shock! It's hard to believe that you are gone! You were so young, full of life and greatly admired! But I also realize that God admired and loved you the most! Even though most of us considered it a loss, it was God that gained. A flower He was looking for, and a beautiful flower He found that day. Though young, you touched a lot of lives, and your home-going celebration proved that. Many lives were changed that day, many to never be the same. Many people are born, live, and die and that ‘s all they have to offer. Yet, you lived, touched lives and changed so many in such a short time! That in itself is awesome! The signifying fact is that your life made a difference in the world and blessed many. I am proud to have been your friend and even more to say that you were mine. I know that you are at peace, but we still miss you! In your youth you did so much, and when God saw that it was good, He called you home. Take care like I know you will, and we all will see you soon!

Your brother and friend
Gerrod D. Stephens

Book Reviews

This is absolutely awe-inspiring! This book gave my faith in God an added boost, knowing of a surety that "to be absent from the body *is* to be present with the Lord." God used you to open your heart and put in writing the events leading up to and beyond the home-going of your loved one. How God must have loved Dee Dee to grant her heart's desire.

Beautiful!
Jeanette Murray-Williams
Full Gospel Holy Temple

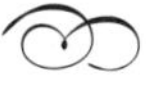

Once you read this book you too will share the emotions, joy and victory that are felt in every page. Reading this book reconfirms God's awesome ability to comfort and lift you in the midst of the storm, letting us all know that we do win in the end, because He is still in control and He's the master of every situation.

Dr. Tony Wade
Full Gospel Holy Temple, Inc.
Minister of Music

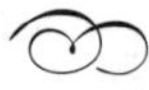

This book is very uplifting, soul stirring, encouraging, and comforting to those who have lost loved ones. In reading the book, it encourages us to realize how mindful God is of His people, and how He will honor their desires.

It is also inspiring for us to know that He will comfort those who are in bereavement, as well as encourage those who are unsaved to seek salvation so that they may see their saved loved ones again. The writer's experience with God during those trying times of sadness, discouragement, and bereavement is incredible and enlightening to anyone who reads this book for the purpose of seeking comfort.

Sis. Lillie Francis
Former instructor
Lobias Murray Christian Academy

This is truly a book for today. It brings consolation, hope and joy as it reaches out to hurting hearts, unlocking spiritual truths.

Heaven is real, and there is a real God full of power, love, understanding, and compassion who cares for us. What a remarkable and beautiful way to show the world what God can do if we have a sweet fellowship with Him and let Him heal our inner hurts. The encounters that the writer experienced expressed both the humanistic as well as the spiritual nature of man as she diligently searched for answers that only God could give.

Not only is this a book filled with hope, encouragement, comfort, strength, and peace but it speaks to us as individuals that we must make preparations now in order to have everlasting life with Christ.

Vivian Carpenter
Former instructor
Lobias Murray Christian Academy

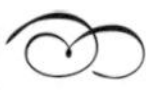

There is nothing like the pain of the loss of a child. I have recently lost two children. The reading of this book has been my second most helpful source of comfort since the death of my son. I know that God is always with me in my low times. The reading of this book has helped me in so many ways. It helped me to remember and showed me how God could bring me through these bad times—I only had to let Him. I think it is a must-read book for anyone who has lost a child in death.

Dorothy Farley
Retired teacher
Lobias Murray Christian Academy

Through the sharing of her personal testimony, Sis. Sandra Wilkerson is a powerful example of being a victor instead of a victim. Her triumph through her belief in God serves as assurance that all things are possible through Him! My soul has been blessed!

Ralph Sanders
Administrator for Greenville, TX ISD

Sis. Wilkerson, thank you for sharing your life-changing experience with me. Oh what an awesome God we serve! Your story is truly inspiring to me, and I am sure it will touch the life of all who read it. As I read page after page of how God dealt with you and helped you and your family to accept the loss of your daughter it brought tears of joy to my eyes…to know that we serve a God who cares so deeply for us!

Again, this book, "your personal testimony," will be of great encouragement to all who read it. May God bless you the more for sharing it with us.

Love,
Your sister in Christ,
Arlene Curl
RN Case Manager

This book is a most touching and moving depiction of a mother's love for her daughter.

Sharon Murray Smith
Principal, Lobias Murray Christian Academy

This book is a tremendous insight into the journey that we travel during the stormy and tumultuous times of bereavement. The author's account sends the reader on a divine revelation of the mercies, grace and faithfulness of our God. This book holds Holy Ghost anointed keys to victory in overcoming the loss of a loved one. Additionally, readers are encouraged by reading how God is a God of promise who honors His word. What a blessing you will experience as you read how God supernaturally manifested His power to the author just when she needed Him most! You will enjoy and be inspired by the unique faith that is exhibited by this "family under fire." This book gives answers and insight into understanding God's providence. This is recommended reading for those who have experienced the loss of a close loved one and those who will have to minster to the bereaved. Truly, the author shows us that you can have peace in the midst of the storm!

Eld. Michael T. Smith
FGHT Ordained Elder

Thank you for sharing your experience in written print. I have literally been able to resolve issues that have so long lingered. You have given us a wealth of encouraging and a beneficial information that will truly help us see God's will in anything. I have truly gained faith and comfort in my own personal quests of life.

Love and respect,
Christine Benson
Early Childhood Education Specialist MAPD

It was such an encouraging story! It brought joy to me to read how God so compassionately eased the unbearable pain of your sorrow (as only He can) in losing such a beautiful young daughter and how He so graciously manifested His continual love to you, while at the same time ministering to you during your healing transition by giving you a "glimpse" of the glory that we all look forward to experiencing one day—the joy that accompanies eternal life with our Savior—which I truly believe that Dee Dee is now enjoying.

Your friend, Clevetta Patterson
Executive Assistant Full Gospel Holy Temple Churches, Inc.

The sincerity and passion displayed in *Memoirs of a Teenage Angel* allows the reader to view the heartache that comes with the loss of a loved one while at the same time providing an intimate portrait of the customized compassion that the Lord shows to each of us. This book will be a blessing to all who read it and will fertilize the seeds of faith and hope to blossom into soul-calming peace for those experiencing grief.

Rev. Dr. Herman L. Murray Jr.
Full Gospel Holy Temple Churches Inc.